Alfred's Premier Piano Course

Dennis Alexander • Gayle Kowalchyk • E. L. Lancaster • Victoria McArthur • Martha Mier

MW01040313

Lesson 3 is available in two versions: Book with CD (#30222) or Book without CD (#27779). Level 3 continues the steady development of artistry and keyboard skills that began in 1A and continued through 2B.

- Note-reading skills are expanded to include ledger-line notes below the bass staff and above the treble staff. The keys of F major and D major are introduced, as well as the chromatic scale.

- Rhythm patterns in 3/8 and 6/8 meter are added to other rhythms of gradually increasing complexity, including patterns that are syncopated or use swing-style eighth notes.

- Technical *Workouts* continue the development of skills, including one-octave scales and chord patterns in the new keys, the waltz bass, and more complex fingering principles.

Lesson Book 3 is designed to correlate with Theory and Performance Books 3 of *Alfred's Premier Piano Course*. When used together, they offer a fully integrated and unparalleled comprehensive approach to piano instruction.

The Book with CD version includes a recording that provides a *performance* model and *practice* companion. Each title is performed twice on acoustic piano—a *performance* tempo and a slower *practice* tempo. See page 49 for information on the CD. A General MIDI Disk 3 (#30426) is available separately.

Edited by Morton Manus

Cover Design by Ted Engelbart
Interior Design by Tom Gerou
Illustrations by Jimmy Holder
Music Engraving by Linda Lusk

ISBN-13: 978-0-7390-4639-5 Book only
ISBN-13: 978-0-7390-5232-7 Book & CD

Contents

2

Premier Music Review

1. Write the counts (by measure) under the notes—then tap and count aloud.

2. Circle the name of the 5-finger pattern. Then play each, using the correct hand.

   a.   C major
        C minor

   b.   G major
        G minor

   c.   A major
        A minor

3. On the blank lines below, name all the notes.

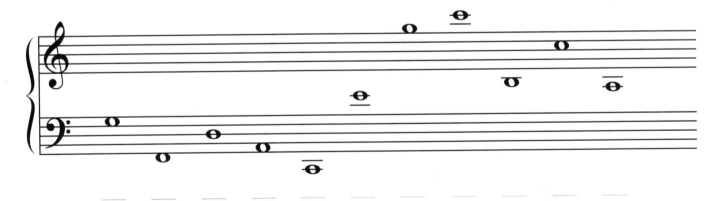

4. Complete the G major scale by writing the missing notes. Then add the key signature in the box.

5. Name each chord by writing the letter name and circling major or minor. Then play.

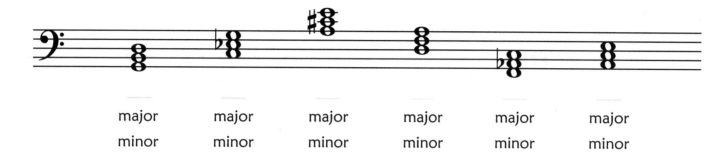

| major | major | major | major | major | major |
| minor | minor | minor | minor | minor | minor |

6. Complete the harmonic intervals by writing the top note.

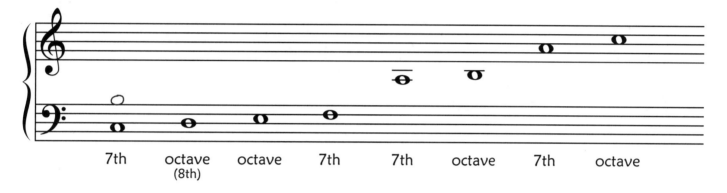

| 7th | octave (8th) | octave | 7th | 7th | octave | 7th | octave |

7. Matching Game: Draw a line from the term or symbol on the left to its matching name or definition on the right.

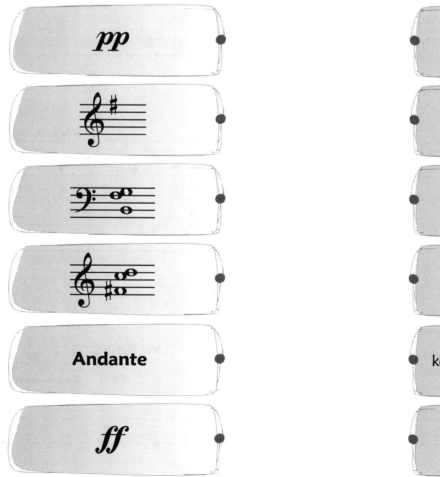
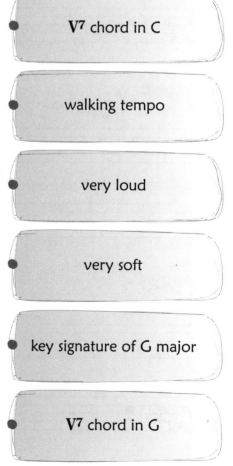

4

Rhythm Workouts

Tap and count aloud 3 times each day.

The Taj Mahal*

CD 1/2 GM 1

* The Taj Mahal is a beautiful palace in India, built by Shah Jahan in memory of his wife.
  It was completed in 1650.

Premier Performer

In measure 1 and similar measures, the notes played by the LH thumb should be softer than those played by finger 5.

Theory Book: page 4

The IV Chord in C

The **IV** chord is built on the 4th note (subdominant) of the scale.

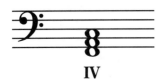

IV

In C major, the **IV** chord often moves F and A up an octave.

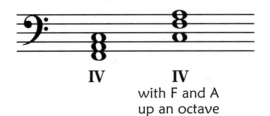

IV   IV
with F and A
up an octave

Moving from the I Chord to the IV Chord

Use these three steps to make **I–IV** in C easier to play,

Step 1: Play the **I** chord.

Step 2: Raise the middle note a half step.

Step 3: Raise the top note a whole step.

The Primary Chords in C

The most important chords in any key are the **I**, **IV** and **V⁷** chords.
They are called the **primary chords.**

1. Play **I**, **IV** and **V⁷**, saying the chord names aloud.

2. Using these rhythms, play **I**, **IV** and **V⁷** in C by reading the chord symbols.

Starting Chord

a. RH

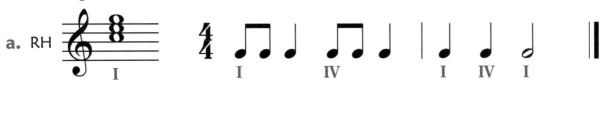

b. LH

The IV Chord in G

The **IV** chord is built on the 4th note (subdominant) of the scale.

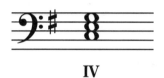

IV

In G major, the **IV** chord often moves C and E up an octave.

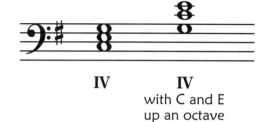

IV   IV
with C and E
up an octave

Moving from the I Chord to the IV Chord

Use these three steps to make **I–IV** in G easier to play,

Step 1: Play the **I** chord.

Step 2: Raise the middle note a half step.

Step 3: Raise the top note a whole step.

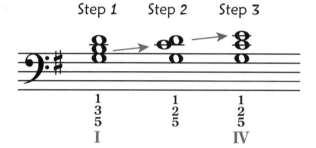

The Primary Chords in G

1. Play **I**, **IV** and **V⁷**, saying the chord names aloud.

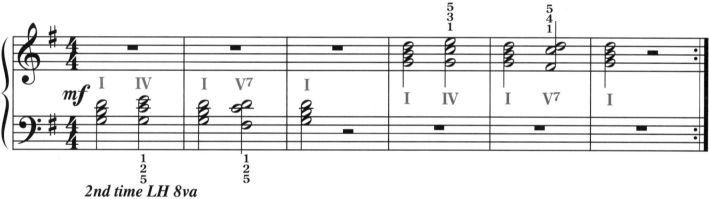

2nd time LH 8va

2. Using these rhythms, play **I**, **IV** and **V⁷** in G by reading the chord symbols.

Starting Chord

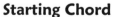

8

Theory Book: page 6
Performance Book: pages 4–5

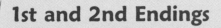

1st and 2nd Endings

1. Play 1st time only, then play again from the repeat sign.

2. Play 2nd time only, skipping 1st ending.

New Rhythm

Tap and count aloud 3 times each day.

Island Daydream

CD 3/4 GM 2

Haitian Folk Song

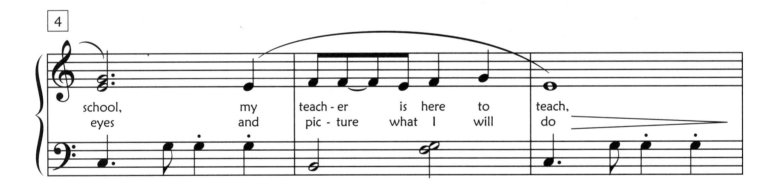

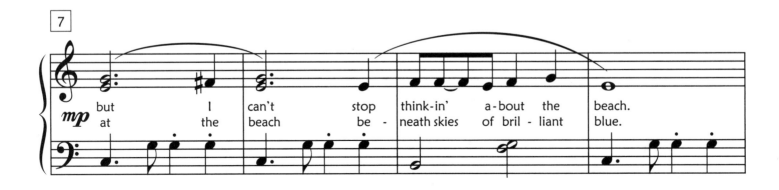

Premier Performer

Transpose the LH of measures 11–19 to G major while your teacher plays the RH.

Workout 1 Changing Fingers

a.

mf

b.

f

Play 3 times each day.

Polovetsian Dance

(from *Prince Igor*)

CD 5/6 GM 3

Alexander Borodin

> **Alexander Borodin** (1833–1887) was a Russian composer who earned a doctoral degree in chemistry. Although trained as a scientist, he composed throughout his lifetime. Several of his works, including the opera *Prince Igor*, were completed by other Russian composers after his death.

Moderately

mp

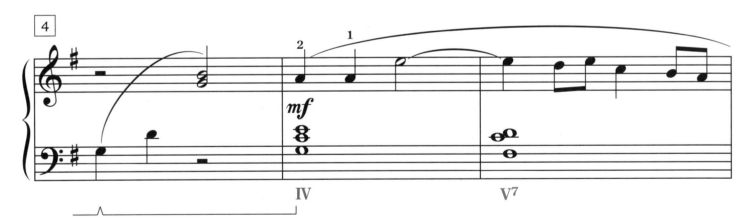

mf

IV

V⁷

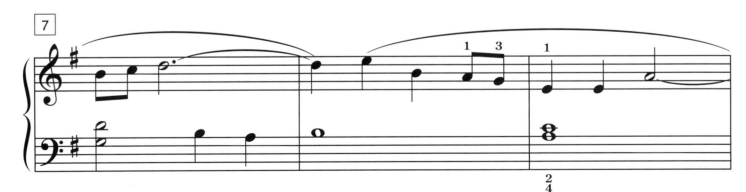

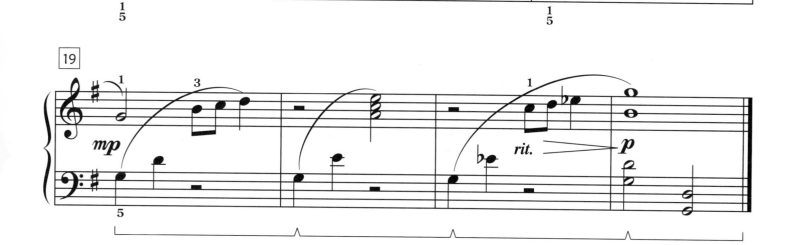

Closer Look · Name the chords (**I, IV** or **V⁷**) for the LH in:

Measure 12 _____

Measure 13 _____

Measure 14 _____

Theory Book: page 8
Performance Book: pages 6–7

Workout 2 LH Fingering Challenge

Play 3 times each day.

Balancing Act

CD 7/8 GM 4

Ludvig Schytte (1848–1909)
Op. 108, No. 12

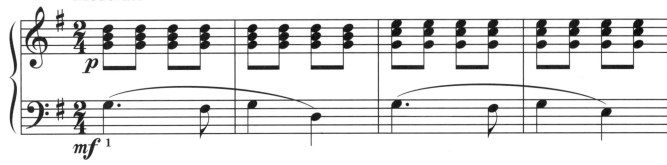

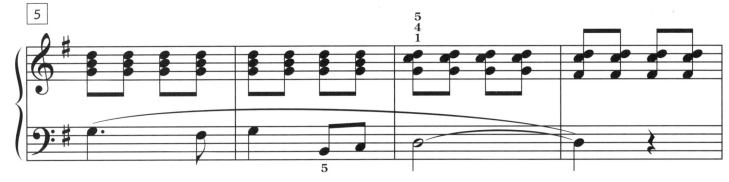

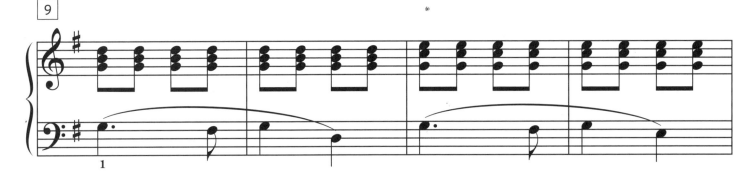

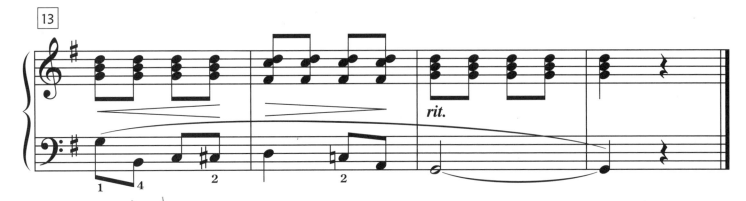

Listen for the perfect balance between the hands by playing the RH chords softer than the LH melody.

Syncopation

Syncopation means to stress a weak beat. In the first measure of the rhythm below, the stress is on beat 2 (rather than beats 1 and 3). The note played on beat 2 is **syncopated** and held until beat 4.

Count: 1 2 – 3 4 | 1 – 2 3 – 4

Tap and count aloud 3 times each day.

New River Train

CD 9/10 GM 5

Traditional

New Rhythm

In the rhythm below, the stress is on the first quarter note. This note is **syncopated**.

Count: 1   + – 2   +   3 – +   4 – +

Tap and count aloud 3 times each day.

New Time Signature

Common Time: $\mathbf{C} = \frac{4}{4}$

Reveille* Boogie

CD 11/12 GM 6

Moderate, with energy

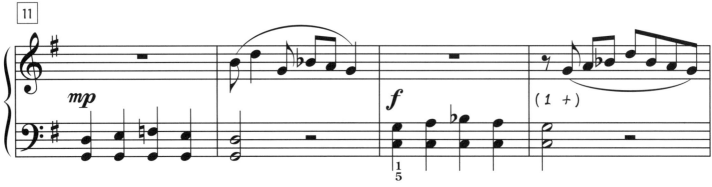

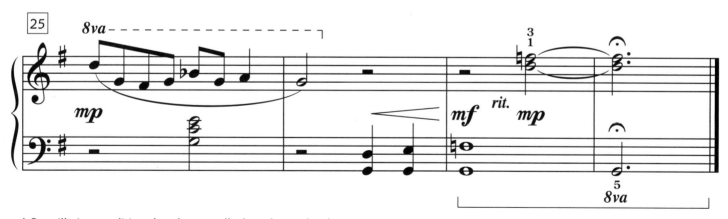

* *Reveille* is a traditional wake-up call played on a bugle.

🔍 **Closer Look** *Circle the* ♪♩ ♪♫♩ *rhythm pattern each time it occurs in Reveille Boogie.*

16

Theory Book: page 11

Swing Style*

Pairs of eighth notes in blues and jazz music are often performed in a long-short rhythm pattern known as *swing style*.

Say: long - short long - short long - short long

Tap and say 3 times each day.

Rhythm Workouts

On your lap, tap and count aloud. First, tap with even eighth notes; then tap in swing style with *long-short* eighth notes.

Down Home Blues

CD 13/14 GM 7

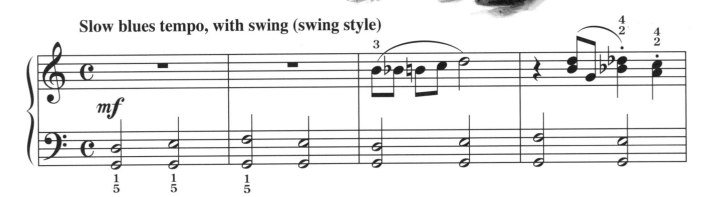

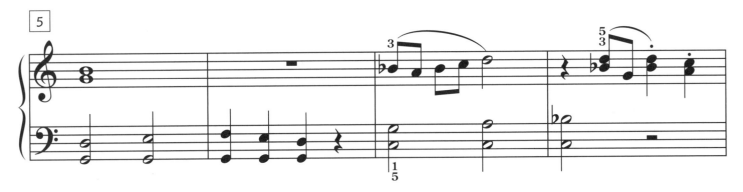

* Note to Teacher: Demonstrate the swing-style rhythms on this page for the student.

Imagination Station

Create a new piece by making up a melody to go with the LH of measures 25–32. Use the notes in the RH G minor 5-finger pattern.

Rhythm Workouts

On your lap, tap each rhythm and count aloud. First, tap with even eighth notes; then tap in *swing* style with *long-short* eighth notes.

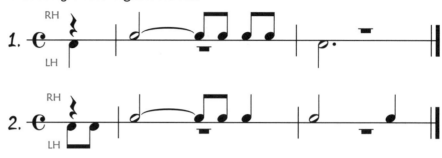

Singin' in the Rain

(from the M-G-M Motion Picture
Singin' in the Rain)

CD 15/16 GM 8

Music by Nacio Herb Brown
Lyric by Arthur Freed

Moderately, with swing (swing style)

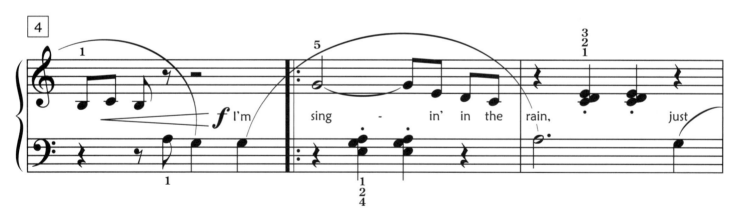

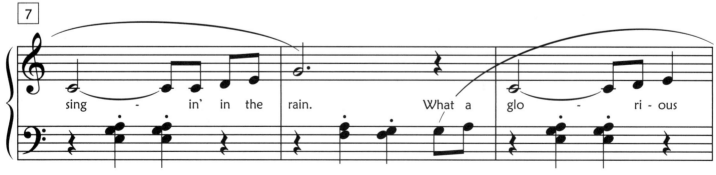

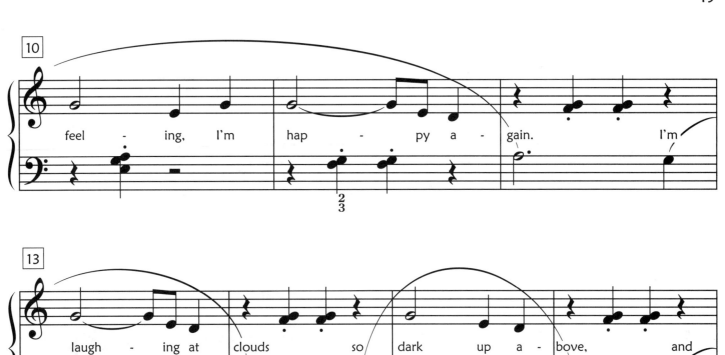

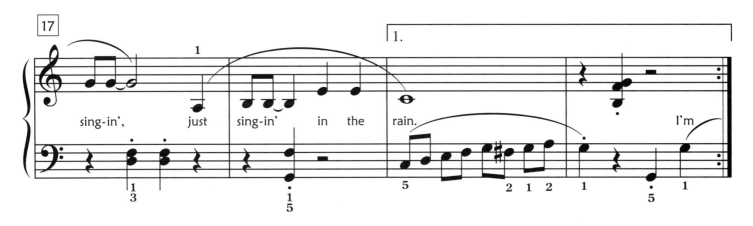

Premier Performer

Listen to bring out the melody as it moves from hand to hand.

Workout 3 **Preparation for F Major Scale**

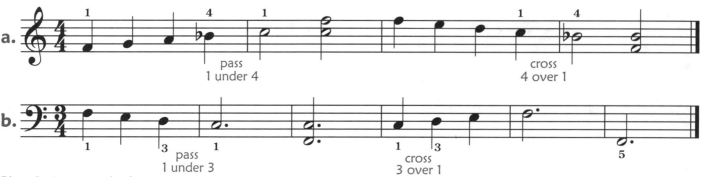

a.
pass
1 under 4

cross
4 over 1

b.
pass
1 under 3

cross
3 over 1

Play 3 times each day.

F Major Scale

The F major scale contains 8 notes—
the F 5-finger pattern + 3 notes.

Half steps occur between notes 3–4 (A–B♭)
and 7–8 (E–F).

In the F major scale, there is one flat—B♭.

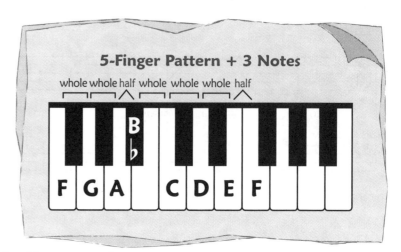

5-Finger Pattern + 3 Notes

whole whole half whole whole whole half

F G A C D E F

Playing the F Major Scale—Hands Separately

Say the finger numbers as you practice slowly. Memorize the fingering.

Right Hand

Repeat 1 octave higher.

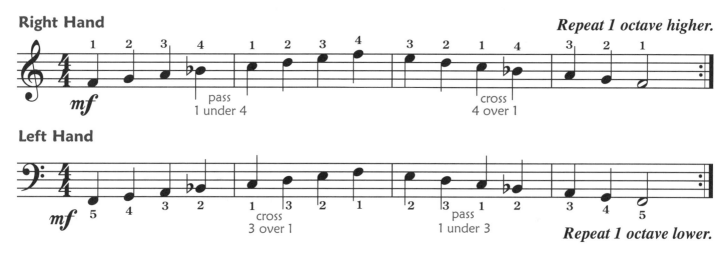

pass
1 under 4

cross
4 over 1

Left Hand

cross
3 over 1

pass
1 under 3

Repeat 1 octave lower.

Note: The fingering for the F major scale in
the LH is the same as C major and G major.
The fingering for the **RH** is **different**.

Workout 4 **Intervals in the F Scale**

2nd   3rd   4th   5th   6th   7th   8th
(octave)

Premier Performer   *Play Workout 4 again one octave lower
with the LH. Begin with finger 5.*

Key Signature of F Major

1. In the F major scale, every B is played flat unless cancelled by a *natural sign*.
2. A piece based on the F major scale is in the key of F major.

Workout 5 LH Ending Pattern

Play 3 times each day.
Transpose to C major.

Minuet in F Major

CD 17/18 GM 9

Leopold Mozart
(1719–1787)

* Students with small hands may omit one note from the octave.

Theory Book: page 15
Performance Book: pages 12–13

The Primary Chords in F

Play **I**, **IV** and **V⁷**, saying the chord names aloud.

2nd time LH 8va

America, the Beautiful

CD 19/20 GM 10

Samuel A. Ward
(1848–1903)

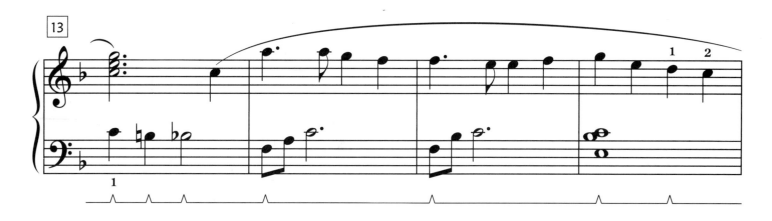

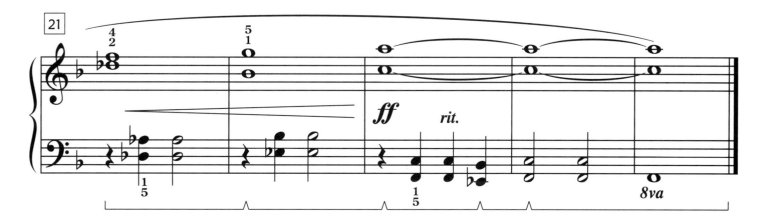

Sight-Reading

Play and count aloud, once each day.

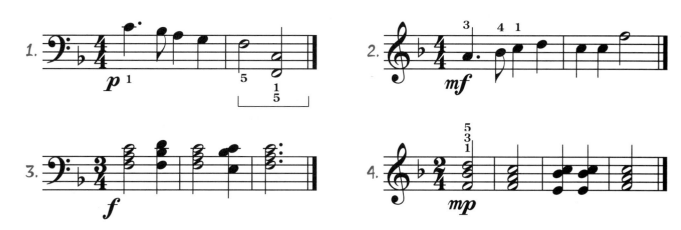

Waltz-Bass Accompaniment

The waltz-bass accompaniment is used in 3/4 time.

Beat 1—play bottom note of chord.

Beats 2 and 3—play middle and top notes together.

Waltz-bass   Block
accompaniment   chord

Play beats 2 and 3 softer than beat 1.

New Italian Term

poco = little

poco rit. = slow down a little

Workout 6 LH Waltz Bass

Play 3 times each day. Transpose to C major.

I   IV   I   V7   I

Ländler in F Major*

CD 21/22 GM 11

Moderato

mf

If you like to waltz,   then   you can thank the

waltz bass

länd - ler.   It's the   folk dance that   start - ed it   all.

broken chord

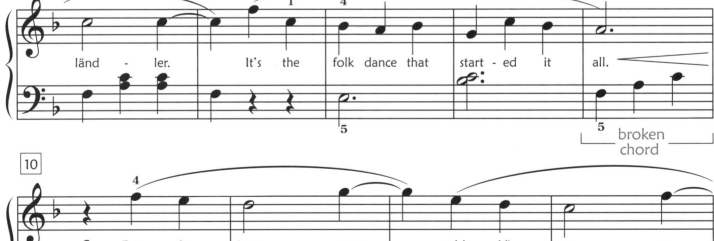

f   From the   inns   near   old Vi - en - na

* A *ländler* is an Austrian folk dance in 3/4 time.

Fine

14

to the pal-ace where it was danced at balls. *mp*

19

p Danc-ing in three quar-ter time while the band plays, cou-ples

23

mp glide a-cross the floor and smile as they sway. E-ven sym-pho-

27

mf nies had länd-ler mel-o-dies. Brahms, Mah-ler,

31

D.C. al Fine

Mo-zart and Hay-dn wrote these. *poco rit.*

Theory Book: page 17

Ledger Lines Below the Bass Staff

Ledger lines below the bass staff are used to notate low notes.

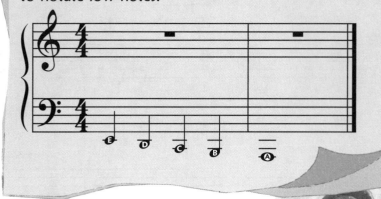

Mystery Theater

CD 23/24 GM 12

Sight-Reading

Play and say note names, once each day.

Ledger Lines Above the Treble Staff

Ledger lines above the treble staff are used to notate high notes.

Sight-Reading

Play and say note names, once each day.

High Wire Acrobats

CD 25/26 GM 13

Moderato

Name notes.

Theory Book: page 19
Performance Book: pages 16–17

Midnight at the Museum

New Italian Term

molto = much, very or **big**
crescendo molto = **big crescendo**

CD 27/28 GM 14

Allegro

At the stroke of 12, that's when the

Name
notes.

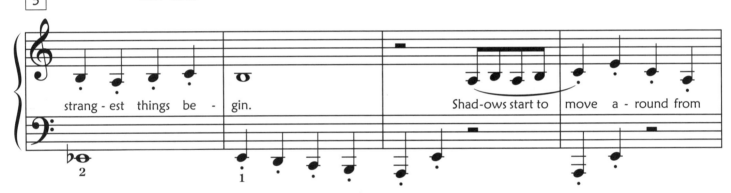

strang-est things be - gin.

Shad-ows start to move a - round from

deep with - in.

cresc. molto
What's that sound from o - ver there?

Be-ing here is quite a scare!

f Got-ta run, got-ta hide from the things in -

Name notes.

Premier Performer

Listen carefully for smooth legato and crisp staccato notes.

The Chromatic Scale

The word *chromatic* means "colorful." This colorful scale is made up entirely of half steps. It uses every key, black and white, and may begin on any key.

Chromatic Scale Fingering

Use 3 on each black key. Use 1 on each white key, except when two white keys are together (E–F and B–C), then use 1–2 or 2–1.

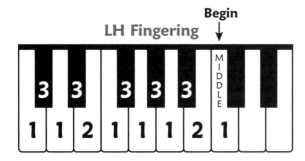

While looking at the keyboard above, play the chromatic scale going *down* and then *up*. Begin on Middle C.

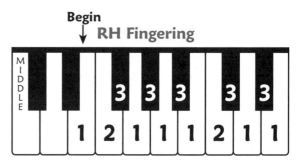

While looking at the keyboard above, play the chromatic scale going *up* and then *down*. Begin on the E above Middle C.

Workout 7 **Chromatic Patterns Using Finger 2**

Play 3 times each day.

Sight-Reading

Play and say note names, once each day.

Tap Shoe Shuffle

CD 29/30 GM 15

Moderate swing tempo (swing style)

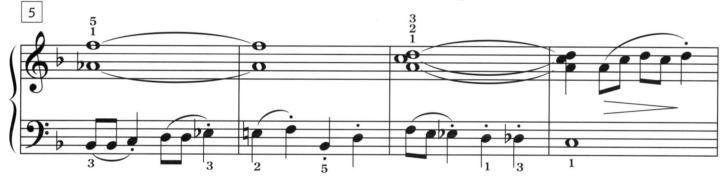

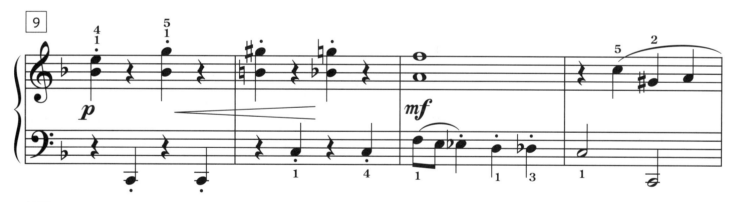

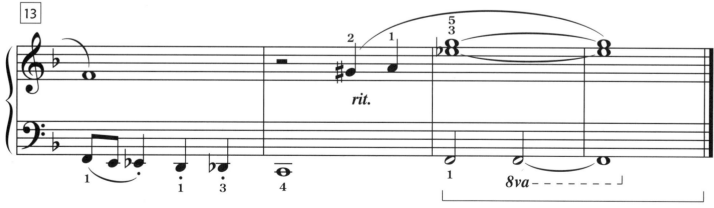

Closer Look *Circle each LH chromatic scale passage going down.*

Painting a Picture with Music Colors

Painters and pianists are similar. Artists paint colorful pictures that can be seen; pianists create colorful sound images that are heard. The piano is capable of many different colors when it is played high or low, loud or soft, quickly or slowly, staccato or legato, and in many other ways.

Color is important in your playing! If all your sounds are alike in color, the playing will not be interesting or appealing to listeners.

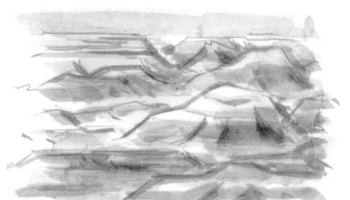

New Tempo Marking

Adagio = *slowly*

The Painted Desert*

CD 31/32 GM 16

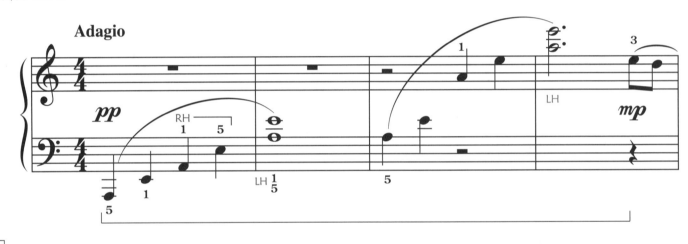

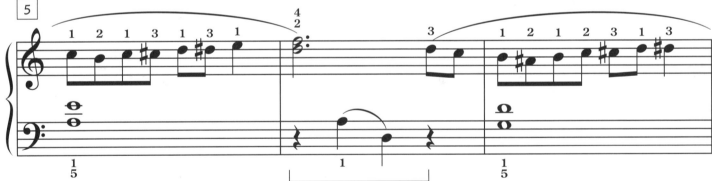

* The Painted Desert, located in Arizona, gets its name from the multi-colored layers of rocks that cover the area.

Premier Performer

Paint a picture with sound in The Painted Desert by:

- Playing the beginning (mm. 1–4) and ending (mm. 21–26) very softly.
- Playing the RH chromatic scale passages very legato.
- Playing the RH louder than the LH in mm. 9–12 and mm. 17–20.

New Time Signature

$\mathbf{3}\over\mathbf{8}$ means 3 counts in every measure.

means an eighth note ♪ gets 1 count.

Note and Rest Values in $\mathbf{3}\over\mathbf{8}$ Time

♪	𝄾	1 count
♩	𝄿	2 counts
♩.	𝄼	3 counts

Tap and count aloud these rhythm patterns.

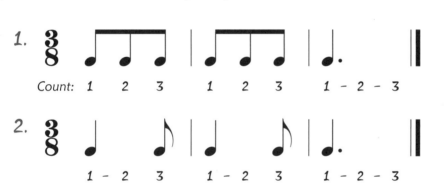

Using these rhythms, play **I**, **IV** and **V⁷** chords in F by reading the chord symbols.

Starting Chord

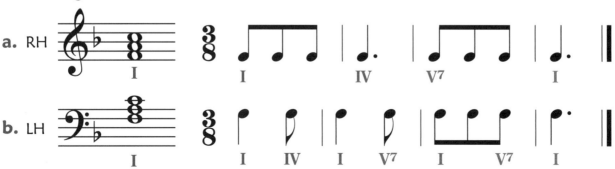

Theory Book: page 24
Performance Book: pages 20–21

Workout 8 Fingering Check

Play 3 times each day.

Morning Sunrise

CD 33/34 GM 17

Cornelius Gurlitt (1820–1901)
Op. 117, No. 13

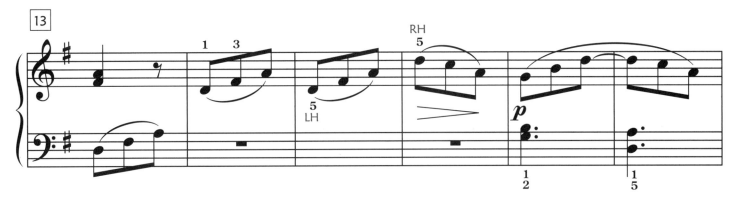

Closer Look Circle each F♯ in Morning Sunrise.

New Time Signature

6 means 6 counts in every measure.
8 means an eighth note ♪ gets 1 count.

Notes and Rest Values in 6/8 Time

♪	┚	1 count
♩	𝄽	2 counts
♩.	𝄽.	3 counts
𝅗𝅥.	▬	6 counts

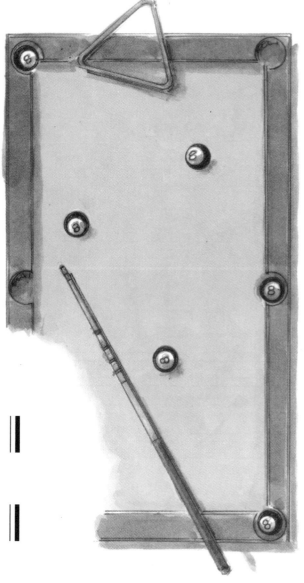

Tap and count aloud these rhythm patterns.

1. **6/8** ♪ ♪ ♪ ♪ ♪ ♪ | ♩. ‖

Count: 1   2   3   4   5   6   1 - 2 - 3 - 4 - 5 - 6

2. **6/8** ♩ ♪ ♪ ♪ | ♩. ‖

1 - 2   3   4 - 5   6   1 - 2 - 3 - 4 - 5 - 6

3. **6/8** ♩. ♩. | ♩ ♪ ♩. ‖

1 - 2 - 3   4 - 5 - 6   1 - 2   3   4 - 5 - 6

Using these rhythms, play **I**, **IV** and **V⁷** chords by reading the chord symbols.

Starting Chord

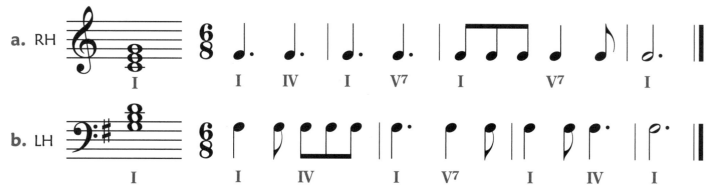

a. RH

I

I   IV   I   V⁷   I   V⁷   I

b. LH

I

I   IV   I   V⁷   I   IV   I

Watercolors

CD 35/36 GM 18

Workout 9 LH Stretch

Play 3 times each day.

Theory Book: page 27
Performance Book: pages 24–25

La Mia Tarantella*

CD 37/38 GM 19

* A *tarantella* is a fast, energetic folk dance from southern Italy.

Premier Performer *Bring out the LH in measures 17–22.*

Workout 10 Preparation for D Major Scale

Play 3 times each day.

D Major Scale

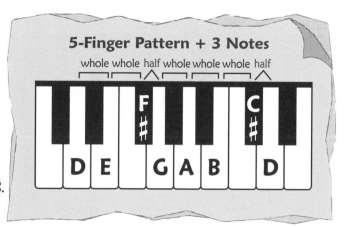

The D major scale contains 8 notes—the D 5-finger pattern + 3 notes.

Half steps occur between notes 3–4 (F♯–G) and 7–8 (C♯–D).

In the D major scale, there are two sharps—F♯ and C♯.

Playing the D Major Scale—Hands Separately

Say the finger numbers as you practice slowly. Memorize the fingering.

Right Hand *Repeat 1 octave higher.*

Left Hand

Repeat 1 octave lower.

Workout 11 Intervals in the D Scale

2nd 3rd 4th 5th 6th 7th 8th (octave)

Premier Performer *Play Workout 11 again one octave lower with the LH. Begin with finger 5.*

Key Signature of D Major

1. In the D major scale, every F and C are played as sharps unless cancelled by a *natural sign*.
2. A piece based on the D major scale is in the key of D major.

Daniel Gottlob Türk *(1756–1813) was a respected German writer of piano teaching pieces. When he was 33 years old, he published Klavierschule (German for "keyboard school"), a piano method that contained separate chapters on learning about note-reading and counting rhythms.*

The Scale Ladder

Daniel Gottlob Türk

Closer Look *Circle the two notes where RH 3 crosses over RH 1; draw a box around the two notes where RH 1 passes under RH 3.*

Duet: Student plays one octave higher.

Alexander/Mier

CD 39/40
GM 20

Theory Book: page 30
Performance Book: page 27

The Primary Chords in D

Play **I**, **IV** and **V⁷**, saying the chord names aloud.

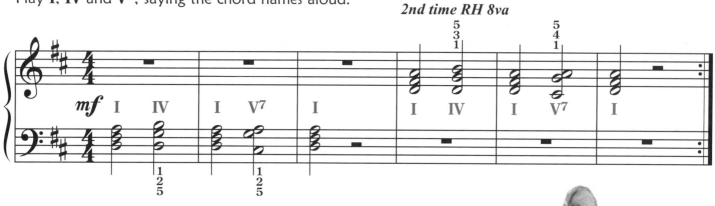

Swingin' the Blues

CD 41/42 GM 21

Moderately, with swing (swing style)

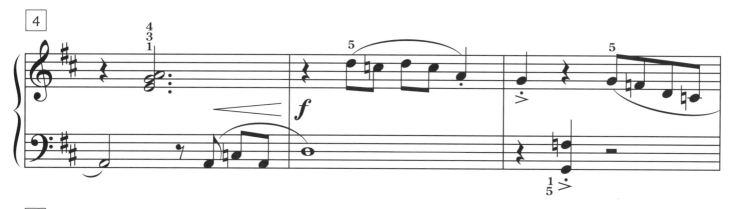

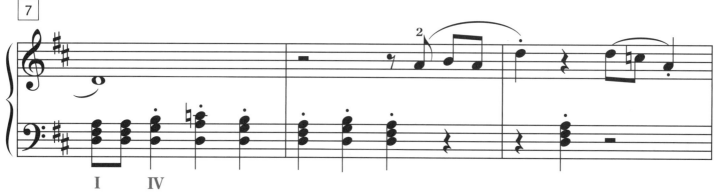

Premier Performer

As you play, listen for the long-short swing style of the eighth notes.

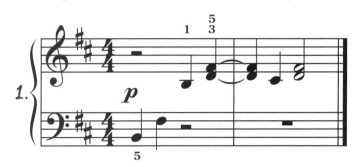

Sight-Reading

Play and count aloud, once each day.

One Moment in Time

CD 43/44 GM 22

Italian Term Review

poco = little

molto = much, **very** or **big**

Moderato

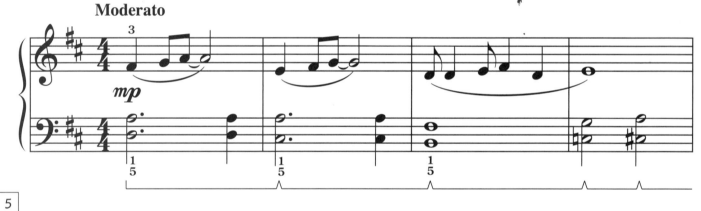

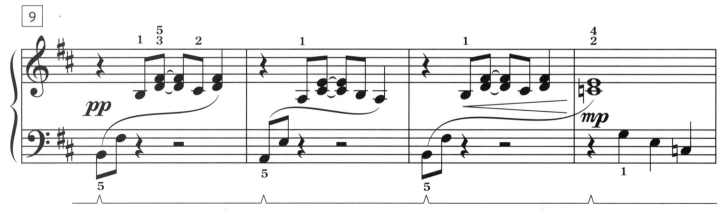

Premier Performer *Let the RH melody sing out above the LH in measures 1–8 and 17–28.*

Celebration Rag

CD 45/46 GM 23

D. C. al Coda

D. C. al Coda is the abbreviation for *Da Capo al Coda*. It means go back to the beginning and play to the small ⊕. Then skip to the *Coda* which means the ending or concluding passage.

With a steady beat

mf

(1 on repeat)

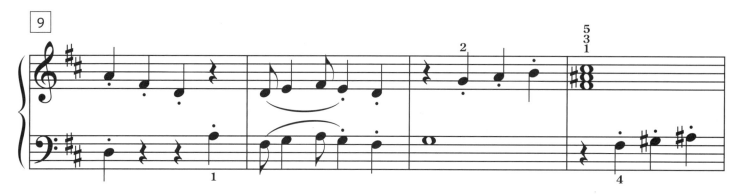

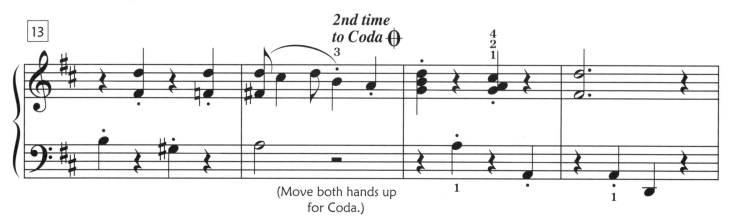

2nd time to Coda ⊕

(Move both hands up for Coda.)

Alfred's

Premier Performer
Piano Achievement Award

presented to

_____
Student

You have
successfully completed
Lesson Book 3
and are
hereby promoted to
Lesson Book 4.

_____ _____
Teacher   *Date*